BEAUTY SALON
COLORING BOOK

MW00958017

HAIR, MAKEUP AND NAILS

ILLUSTRATED BY TC MAHALA

This coloring book was created with the idea of helping you visualize different looks and combinations of hair colors, styles, makeup, and nails. It was also created with multiple duplicates of each illustration for you to be creative and see different variations with the same model.

For updates on other products, like us on Facebook @ **Pickled Genius Projects**

PICKLED GENIUS PROJECTS

HAIR COLOR

MAKEUP & NAILS

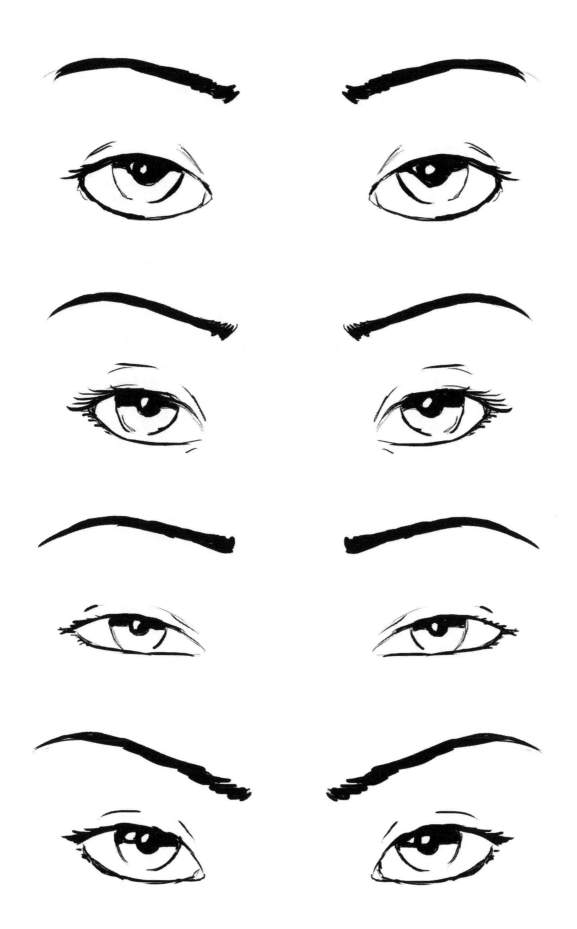

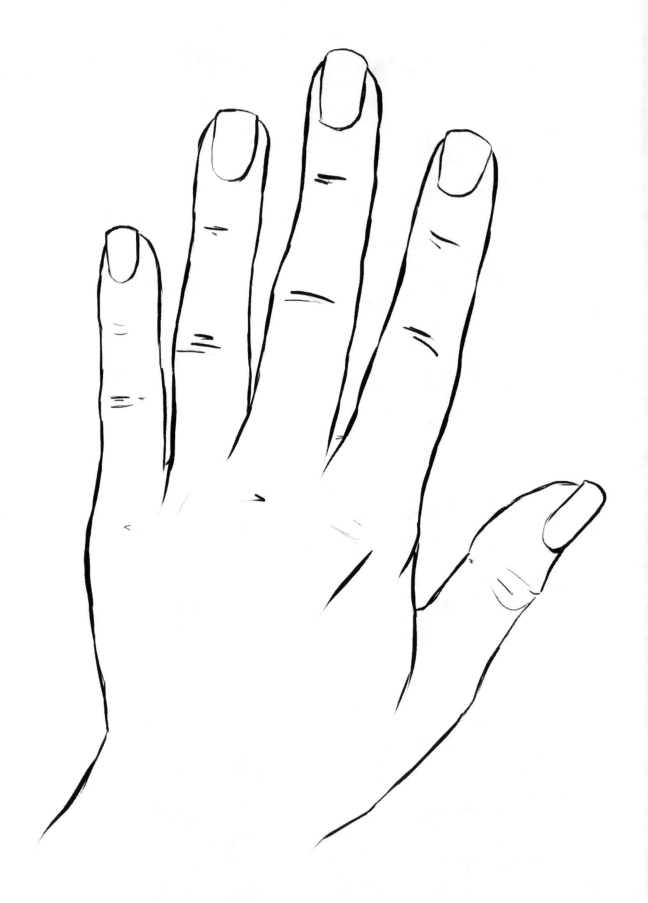

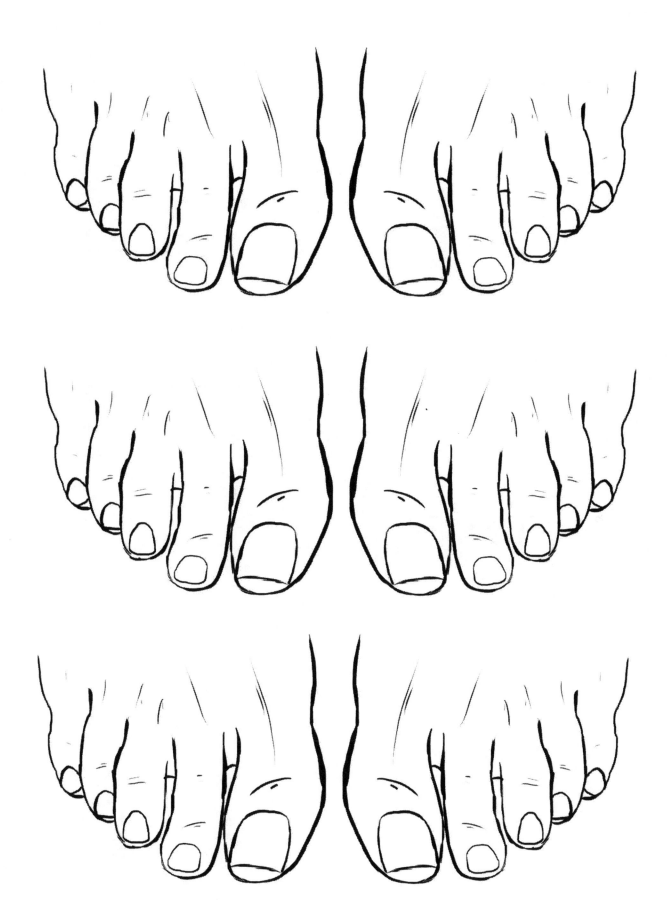

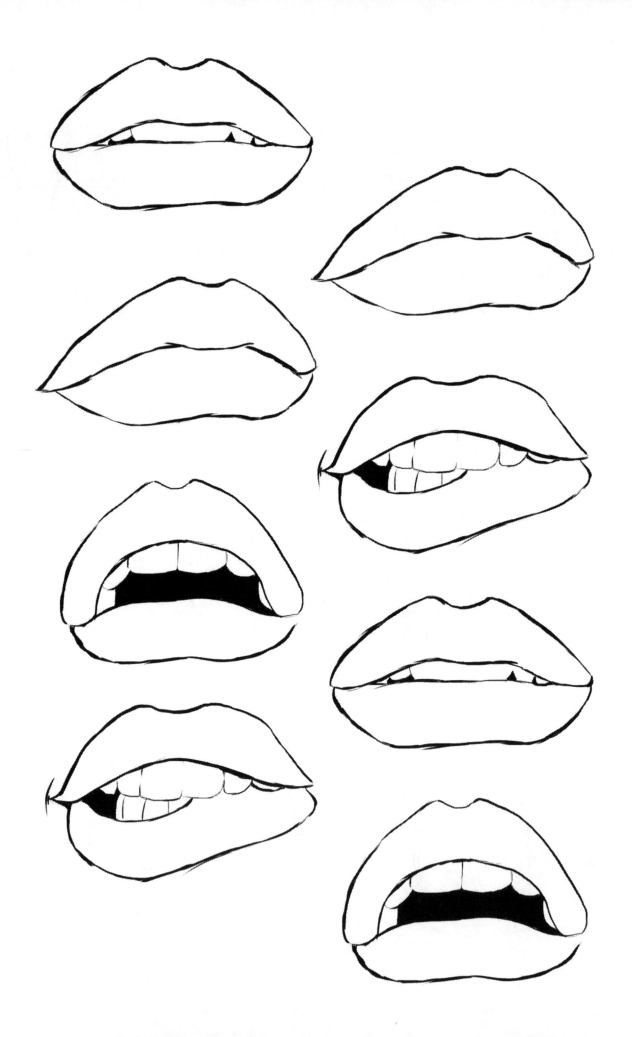

HAIR STYLE

HAIR COLOR

MAKEUP & NAILS

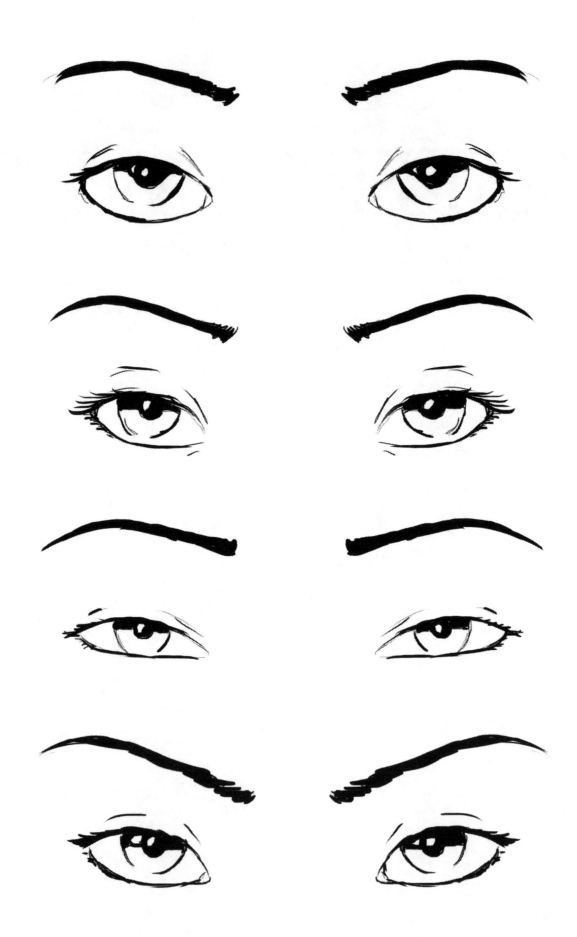

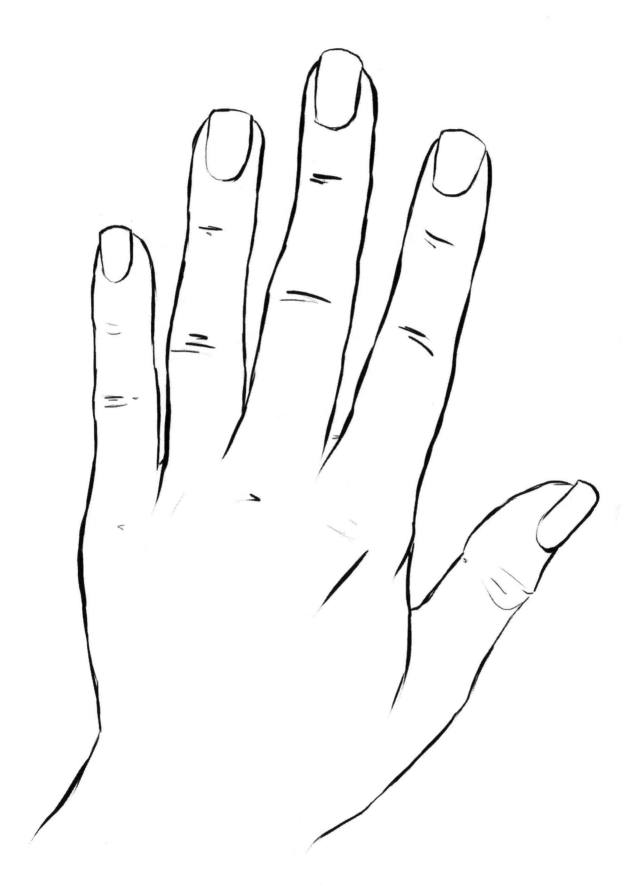

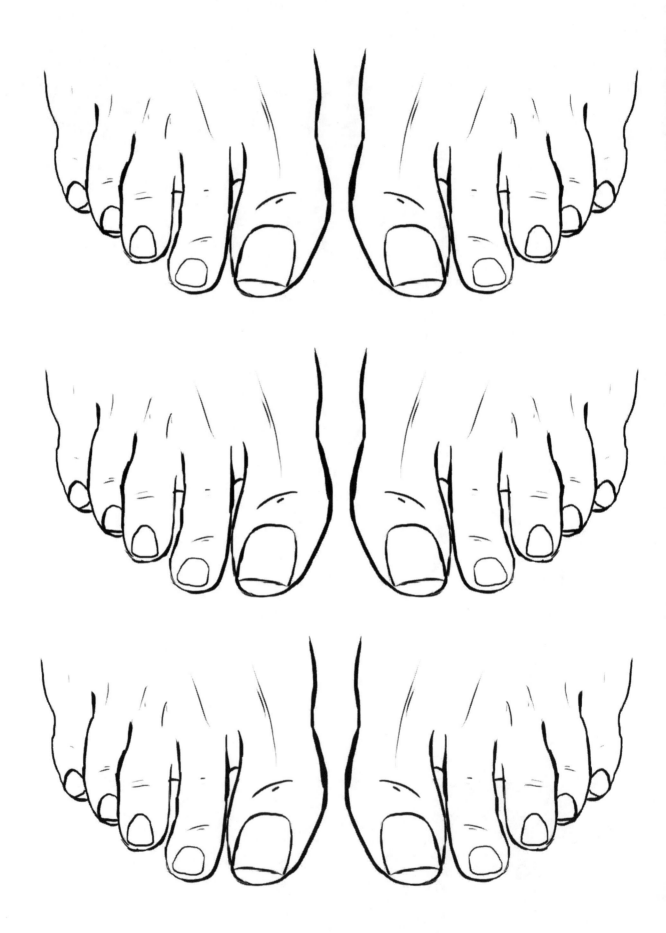

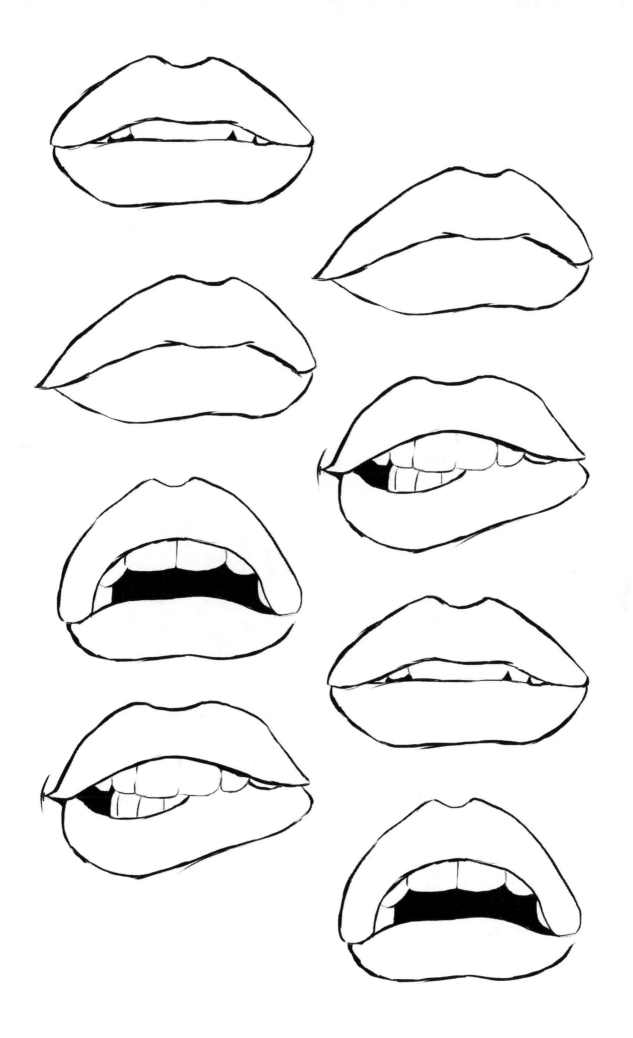

HAIR STYLE

HAIR COLOR

MAKEUP & NAILS

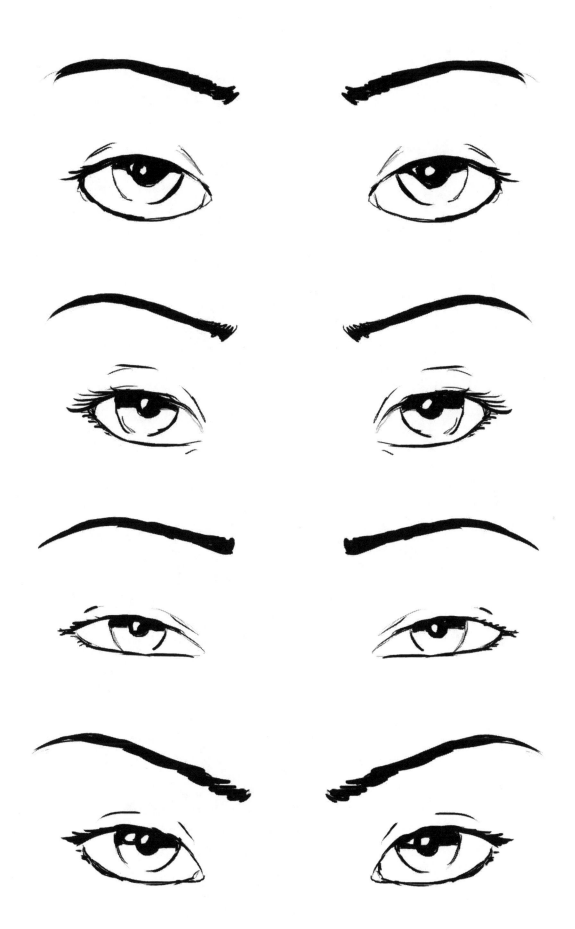

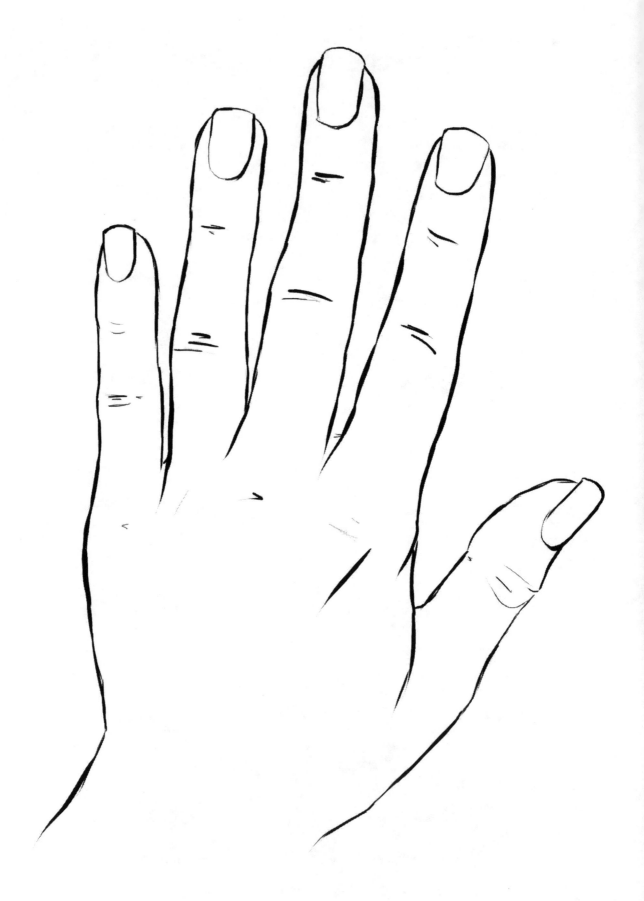

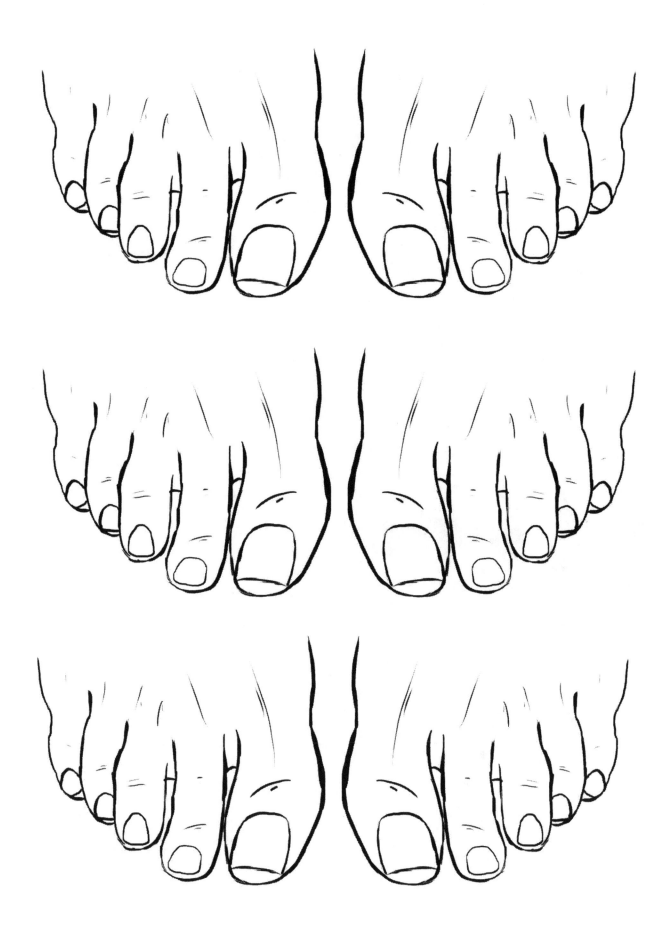

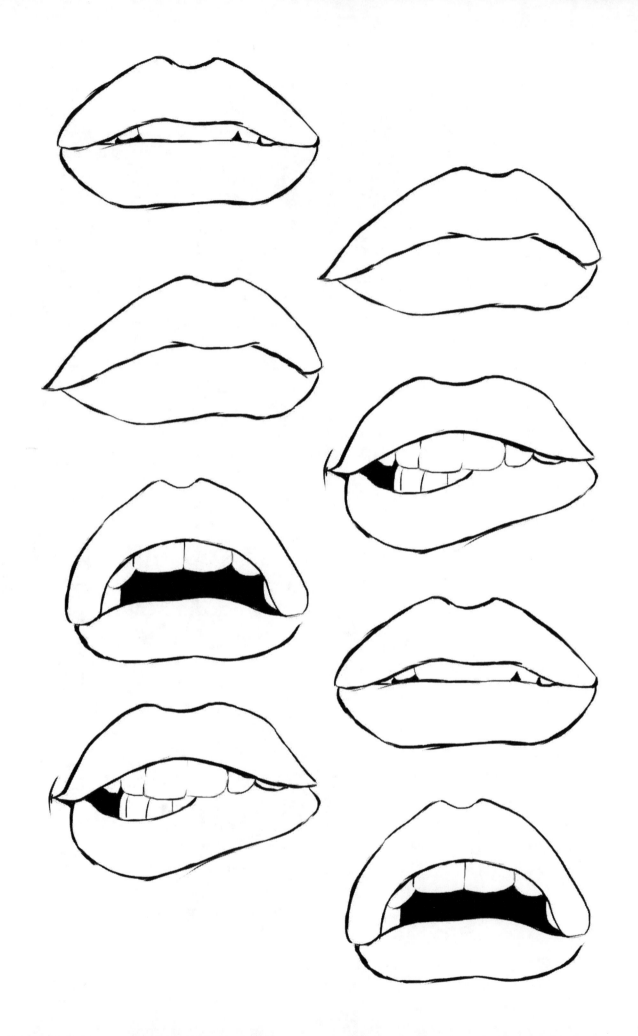

HAIR STYLE

HAIR COLOR

MAKEUP & NAILS

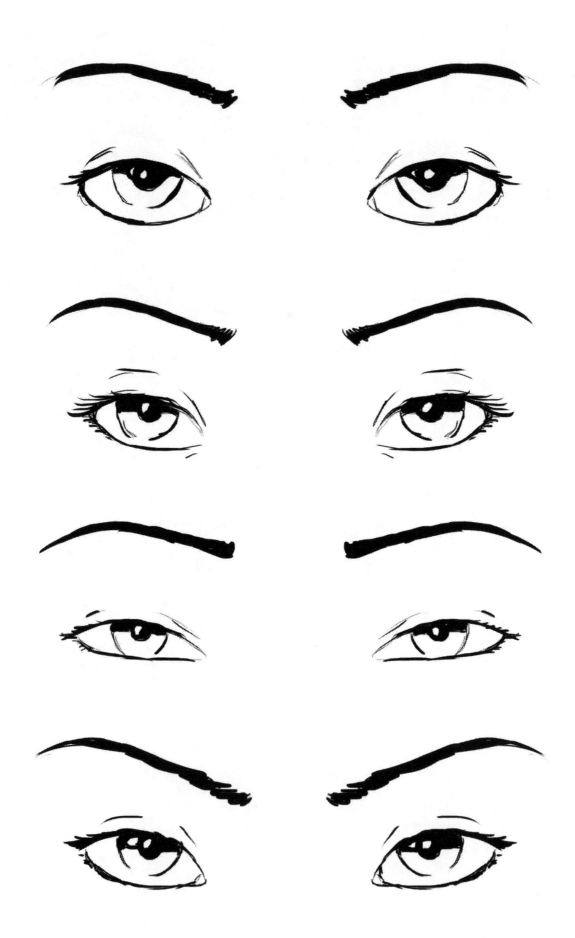

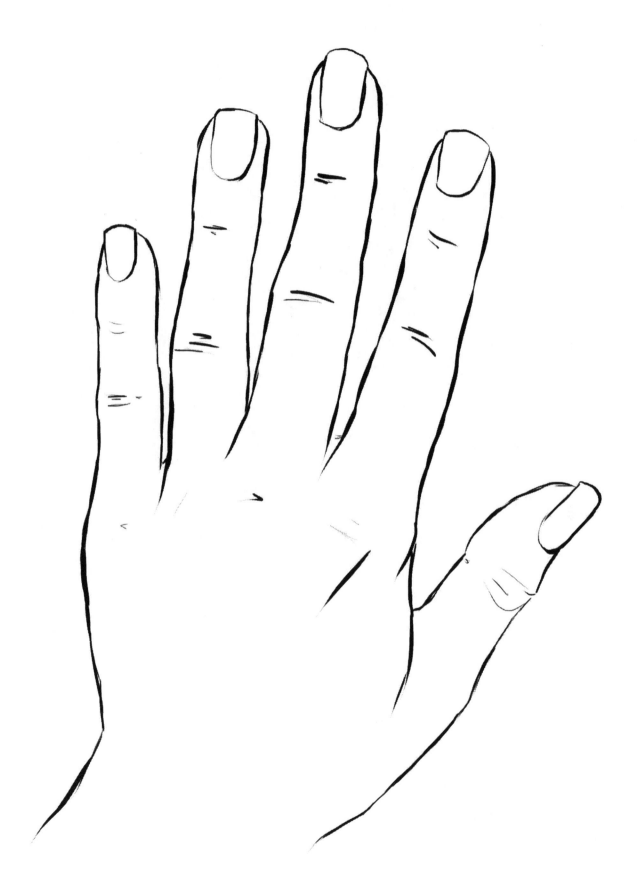

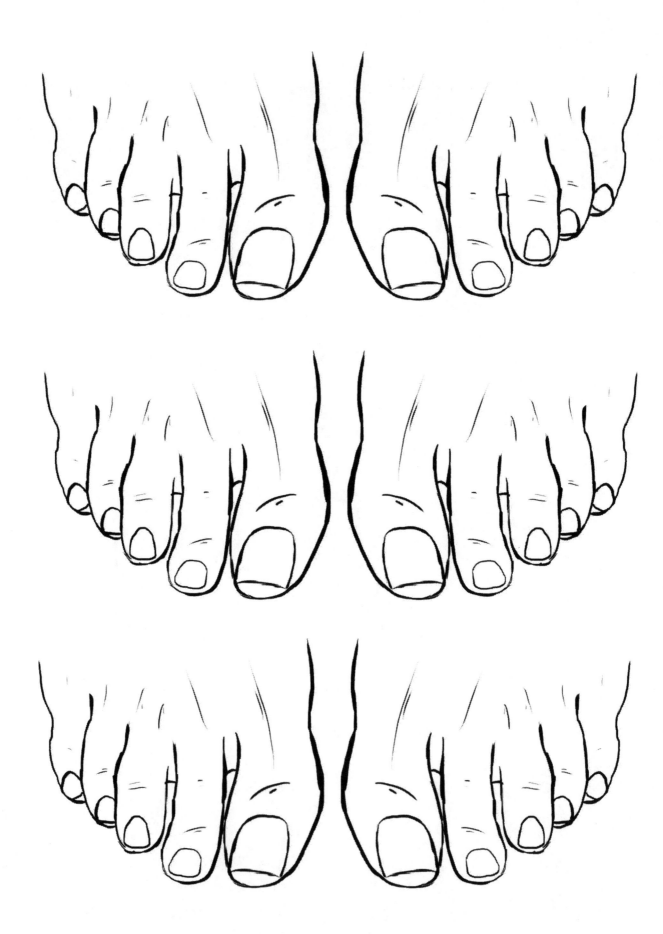

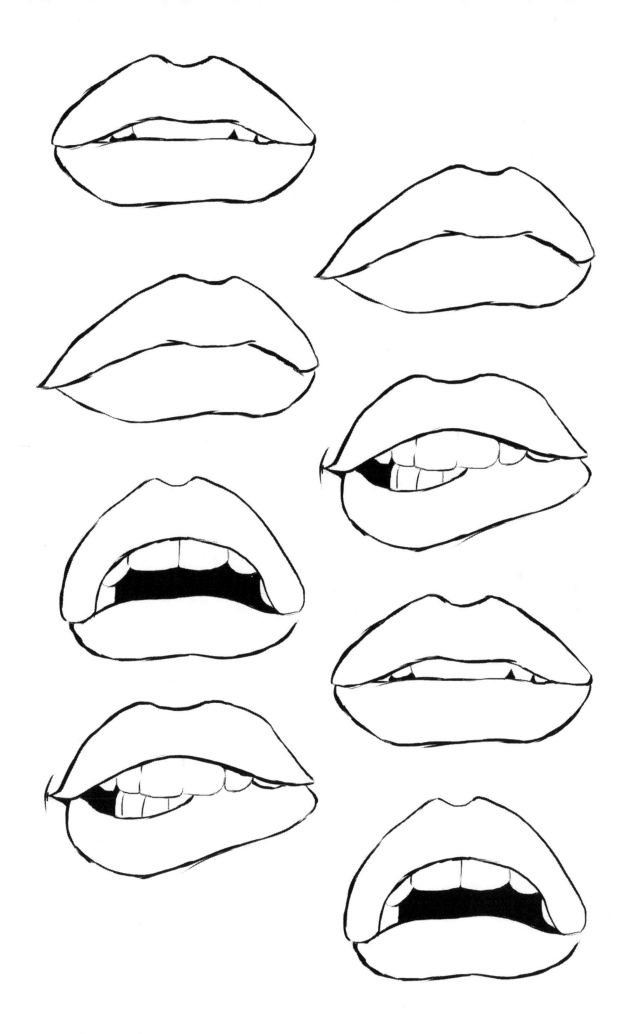

HAIR STYLE

HAIR COLOR

MAKEUP & NAILS

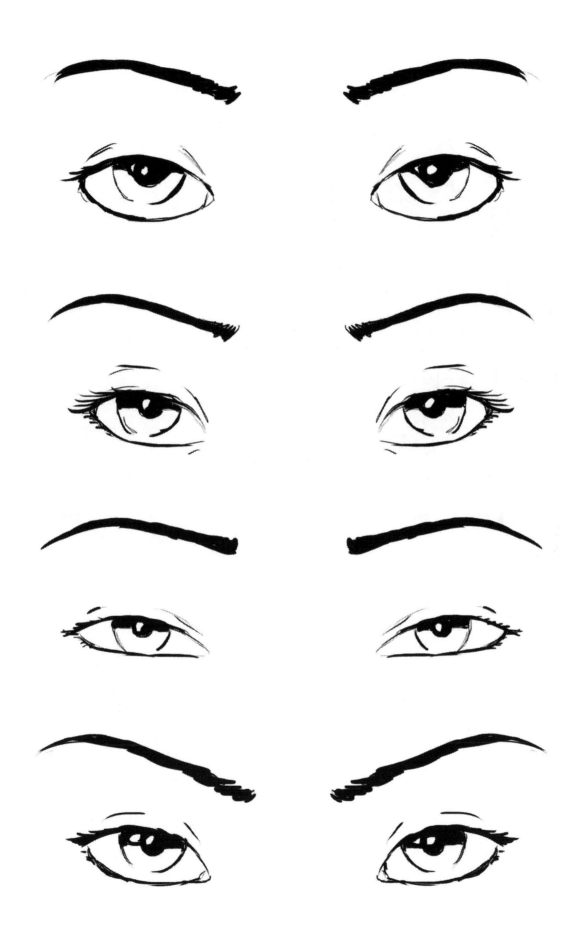

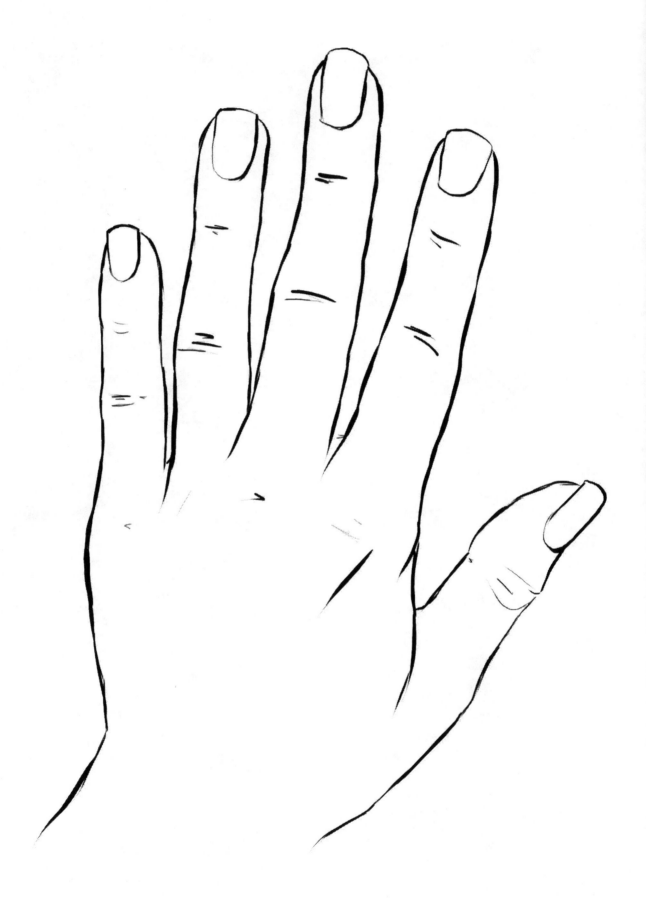

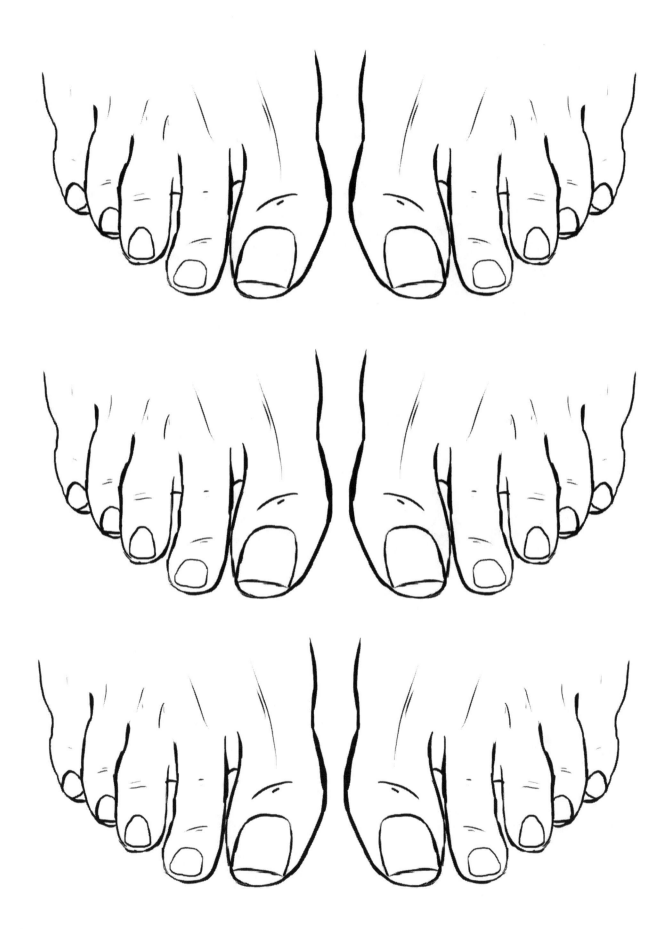

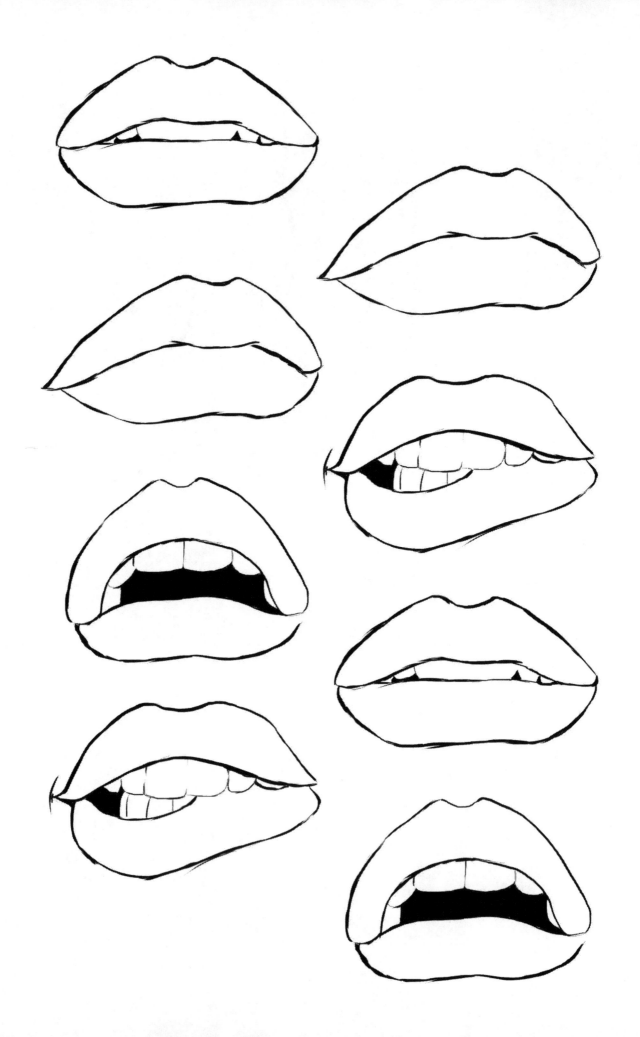

HAIR STYLE

Made in the USA
Las Vegas, NV
24 November 2023

81411213R00061